1st Grade Reading and Skills Practice with Favorite Bible Stories

# Mighty
# Reader
# Workbook

Grade 1

written by
## Heidi Cooley

B&H KIDS
EVERY little WORD MATTERS
BHKids.com

## Dedication

*For Jeff:* My dear husband and biggest fan, thank you for believing in me and encouraging me to take on this project!

*For Savannah and Shepard:* Thank you for your patience and support during the writing process!

*For my parents:* Thank you for the endless examples of creativity, doing BIG things for the Lord, and having the courage to try new things in life.

*For my students:* Your hard work and dedication will take you on many reading adventures!  Keep up the good work!

Scripture quotations are taken from the Christian Standard Bible®,
Copyright © 2017 by Holman Bible Publishers.
Used by permission. Christian Standard Bible® and CSB® are
federally registered trademarks of Holman Bible Publishers.

DEWEY: C372.4
SUBHD: READING \ READING READINESS \
BIBLE--STUDY AND TEACHING

Printed in Shenzhen, Guangdong, China in February 2018
1 2 3 4 5 6 • 22 21 20 19 18

# Dear Parents,

During my thirteen years of teaching, I have learned the importance of daily reading and the impact it has on a child's learning development. Although your child reads a lot in the classroom, he or she needs an additional twenty minutes of reading at home as well. So it's crucial that you become a reading partner. Parents constantly ask me, "How can I help my child with reading? What should he be reading? What questions do I ask her after she has read?" These questions gave me the idea of using God's Word to practice the reading standards and skills your child learns in the classroom. It's a way of ending your child's day with reading practice *and* Bible learning!

In the *Mighty Reader Workbook*, I offer thirteen week-long lessons, each focusing on one story for six days. Your child will read the story in a different way each day and will be asked different questions. Be sure to refer to the Reading Strategies Guide on page 6 to understand how you will read with your child. The lessons will be similar throughout the book, which provides your child with the repetitive structure necessary for extra reading practice and gaining fluency.

Encourage your child to read aloud the questions to you. If he struggles, help him with the words. Also encourage him to look back in the text for answers, which is a skill he is learning in school. I've created questions for each lesson that align with the reading skills and standards taught in first grade. The questions include verbiage your child should be familiar with from his teacher. This workbook is not designed for your child to do alone. It is geared for parents as partners. Partner with your child to create a better reader!

As a parent, I know how difficult it can be to get homework completed each night and try to have a devotional time with your child too. My goal is to help your child complete the suggested twenty minutes of reading each night in God's Word and get skills practice too! I hope you enjoy the *Mighty Reader Workbook*!

Blessings,

Heidi Cooley

# Contents

## New Testament Stories

# Reading Strategies Guide

Every week, your child is introduced to a new Bible story to be read using a different strategy each day. This repetition helps increase reading fluency, the ability to read text smoothly and accurately.

- Echo Read. The adult reads one or two sentences aloud, and then the child repeats those same sentences. Encourage the reader to touch each word as he reads aloud.

- Choral Read. The adult and the child read the story at the same time. Encourage the child to track the words with her finger in a continuous motion as she reads along.

- Cloze Read. The adult begins reading the story aloud and pauses on a specific word in each sentence to allow the child to fill in the word that comes next.

- Partner Read. The adult reads a sentence or paragraph aloud, and then the child reads the next sentence or paragraph aloud. Encourage the child to track the words with her finger.

- Independent Read. The adult listens to the child read aloud the text independently. If a child gets stuck on a word, ask him to try to sound out the word. Give clues if necessary in order to move onto the next word.

- Fluency Check. The adult sets the timer for one minute and asks the child to read the passage as quickly as possible. Once the timer is done, the adult counts the words read correctly to see how many the child reads in one minute. (See "Reading Skills Guide" on the next page.)

# Reading Skills Guide

- Key Details. This area assesses a child's comprehension of the passage by asking him to read and identify different key details such as main idea; character/setting; problem/solution; cause/effect; who, what, when, where, why, and how questions; and sequencing the events.

- Visualization. With this skill the child will create a picture in his mind to demonstrate comprehension. Drawing a picture is one way to practice and demonstrate understanding of the text.

- Text Features. This skill connects to non-fiction text. The student practices or locates items in the text such as labels, headings, bold print, and captions.

- Context Clues. With this skill the reader will determine the meaning of words and multiple-meaning words based on the context of the sentence or passage.

- Phonics. This skill allows students to work with words and their sounds.

- Connecting Writing with Reading. A writing component is connected to the passage each week. The child is asked to write a response to the passage. Encourage him to use correct punctuation and letter formation. Reading and writing go hand in hand, and both are necessary to become a strong reader.

- Fluency. Each lesson is designed to last around twenty minutes and have the child read each day. Repetition is one of the keys to increasing reading fluency and is practiced in the daily lessons. The goal for a first grader is to read 52 WPM (words per minute) on grade-level text by the end of first grade. To practice, set the timer and have your child read the passage for one minute. Count the words read correctly to get an idea of where your child's ability lies.

- Decoding. This skill asks the students to decode or sound out a word. It's critical that the reader know her letter sounds to be able to decode correctly.

# Noah and the Ark

## *Vocabulary*

The list of words below will be in the story. Take a few minutes to discuss the meanings of these words with your child before beginning to read. Ask your child to repeat them to you and use them in a sentence.

**righteous:** in a right relationship with God

**sinning:** not obeying God

**massive:** very large

**dove:** a type of bird

**promise:** a statement that you will do something

**obey:** to follow someone's commands

Biblical terms: **Noah, ark**

## *Skills*

Refer to the Reading Skills Guide on page 7 for a detailed explanation about many of these skills.

| | |
|---|---|
| Comprehension Questions | Visualization |
| Context Clues | Synonyms |
| Inferencing | Connecting Writing with Reading |
| Key Details | Text Features—Captions |
| Problem/Solution | Vocabulary |

# Noah and the Ark

*from Genesis 6:1–9, 17*

1. Long ago there lived a man named **Noah**. He was a **righteous** man because he obeyed God. The other people around him were **sinning**. This made God upset.

2. He told Noah to build an **ark**, a big boat. The ark reached up high in the sky. It had many rooms for the animals. God told Noah to bring every kind of animal onto the ark. Noah and his family went on the ark too.

3. God sent a **massive** flood. The water covered all the earth. It lasted forty days and nights. Only Noah and his family were left.

4. Later, Noah sent out a **dove**. It came back with an olive branch. This meant the water was drying up!

5. Soon, Noah and his family left the ark. The animals got off too. Noah thanked God for keeping them safe. God put a rainbow in the clouds as a **promise**. The earth would never again be flooded.

6. Noah obeyed God. You can **obey** God too. God keeps His promises. Have you ever made a promise? If you make a promise, be sure you keep it.

**Mighty Reader, remember Noah the next time you see a rainbow on a rainy day.**

9

# Day 1

## Skills: Comprehension, Context Clues

1. Read the story as an *echo read* with someone in your home.

2. Reread paragraph 2. What did God ask Noah to do? Underline evidence in yellow to show where you found your answer. Write your answer in the box.

3. What do you think the word righteous means? Circle the word righteous in (blue) in the text.

4. What does the word massive mean in the following sentence? *God sent a massive flood.* Write your answer in the box.

# Day 2

❶ Read the story as a *choral read* with someone in your home.

❷ Reread paragraph 4. What did Noah do to check for dry land? Write it in the box.

❸ What is the *problem* in paragraph 1? Underline the sentence in <u>red</u> that tells you the problem. Write the problem in the box.

❹ What is the *solution* in paragraph 3? Underline the sentence in <u>green</u> that tells you the solution. Write the solution in the box.

# Day 3

**1** Read the story as a *cloze read* with someone in your home.

**2** Reread paragraph 5. What did God do to show He would never flood the earth again? Write it in the box.

_(empty box)_

**3** What does the word **promise** mean?

O a lie
O a statement that you will do something
O a story

**4** <u>Underline</u> the word **rainbow** in paragraph 5 and use your writing tools to draw a picture of a rainbow in the box below.

_(empty box)_

# Day 4

1. Read the story as a *partner read* with someone in your home.

2. Read this sentence: *God told Noah to build an ark.*
Write a *synonym*, or a word that means almost the same thing as **ark**, in the box below.

3. Reread paragraph 4. What kind of bird did Noah send out? Write it in the box.

4. What did the bird bring back to show the water was drying up? Circle the answer in the text and write it in the box.

# Day 5

## Skills: Connecting Writing with Reading

1   Read the story as an *independent reader* to someone in your home. You can do it! Ask someone for help if you get stuck on a word.

2   Respond to the reading through *writing*. Don't forget to use the correct punctuation in your sentences and try to add some detail words too.

On the lines below, write about the following questions: What is your favorite animal? Which animal would you want to take care of on the ark and why?

_____

_____

_____

_____

_____

_____

_____

Make it your goal to write at least three sentences. After you finish your sentences, read them aloud to someone in your home.

# Day 6

Use your writing tools to *draw and color a picture* of the ark in the box below. After drawing your picture, write a *caption* under your illustration.

Write your caption in the box below.

## Fluency Check

Set the timer for one minute and see how many words in the passage you can read correctly. You are a Mighty Reader!

# Jonah and the Great Task

## *Vocabulary*

The list of words below will be in the story. Take a few minutes to discuss the meanings of these words with your child before beginning to read. Ask your child to repeat them to you and use them in a sentence.

**task:** a job or mission

**great:** large or important

**fierce:** having a lot of power or strength

**enormous:** very large

**sinning:** not obeying God

**trust:** to have faith in something

**courage:** bravery

Biblical terms: **Jonah**, **God**, **Nineveh**

## *Skills*

Refer to the Reading Skills Guide on page 7 for a detailed explanation about many of these skills.

Comprehension Questions

Context Clues

Multiple Meanings

Key Details

Repetition

Visualization

Connecting Writing with Reading

Text Features—Labels

Vocabulary

# Jonah and the Great Task

*from Jonah 1:1–3:10*

**1** **Jonah** was a man chosen by **God**. He was given a great **task**. He was told to go to **Nineveh** to warn the people about their sin. He was scared, so he ran away.

**2** He got on a ship and sailed away from Nineveh. God sent a **fierce** storm! Jonah knew he could not hide from God. He knew what he had to do.

**3** He told the men on the ship to throw him into the sea. He sank down, down, down into the water. God sent an **enormous** fish to swallow Jonah up. It was dark and stinky inside the belly of the fish. Jonah prayed to God. He told God he was sorry. Three days later, the fish spit Jonah out onto dry land!

**4** God told Jonah to go to Nineveh again. This time Jonah obeyed. He told the people to stop **sinning**. They chose to obey too!

**5** Jonah learned to **trust** God. You can trust God too. He can use all kinds of people to do great tasks. He can even use you. He will give you **courage**. Remember the story of Jonah when you have a great task someday. God loves you.

**God will always be with you, Mighty Reader!**

# Day 1

*Skills: Comprehension, Context Clues, Multiple Meanings*

1. Read the story as an *echo read* with someone in your home.

2. What did God ask Jonah to do? Write your answer in the box. Underline evidence in the text in yellow to show where you found your answer.

```
[                                                                    ]
```

3. What do you think the word **task** means? Write your answer in the box.

```
[                                                                    ]
```

4. What does the word **great** mean in the following sentence? *He was given a great task.* Write your answer in the box.

```
[                                                                    ]
```

# Day 2

*Skills: Key Details, Context Clues*

**1** Read the story as a *choral read* with someone in your home.

**2** Reread paragraph 3. What did Jonah have to do to stop the storm? Write your answer in the box.

**3** What is the setting in paragraph 3? Underline the sentence in <u>red</u> that tells you the setting. Write your answer in the box.

**4** Circle the word in (green) that means "not obeying God." Write the word in the box below.

# Day 3

1. Read the story as a *cloze read* with someone in your home.

2. Reread paragraph 3. What did Jonah do when he was inside the belly of the fish? Write your answer in the box.

3. There is some evidence of repetition, words that are repeated, in paragraph 3. Circle in (blue) the words that are repeated.

4. Underline the words enormous fish in paragraph 3. Use your writing tools to draw a picture of an enormous fish in the box below.

# Day 4

## Skills: Context Clues

1. Read the story as a *partner read* with someone in your home.

2. Reread paragraph 5. Fill in the missing words from the following sentences:

   Jonah learned to _____ God. You can trust _____ too!

3. What do you think the word **fierce** means in the following sentence? *God sent a fierce storm!* Write your answer in the box.

   _____

4. What do you think the word **courage** means in the following sentence? *He will give you courage.* Write your answer in the box.

   _____

# Day 5

## Skills: Connecting Writing with Reading

1 Read the story as an *independent reader* to someone in your home. Ask someone for help if you get stuck on a word. Try your best!

2 Respond to the reading through *writing*. Don't forget to use the correct punctuation in your sentences, and try to add some detail words too.

On the lines below, write about what you think it would have been like to be on the boat with Jonah during the fierce storm.

_____

_____

_____

_____

_____

_____

_____

Make it your goal to write at least 3 sentences. After you finish your sentences, read them aloud to someone in your home.

# Day 6

*Skills: Illustrations and Comprehension, Text Features*

Use your writing tools to *draw and color* a picture of the ship with Jonah and the storm. After drawing your picture, *label* different parts of your picture. Try to include words such as *ship, clouds, waves, rain, Jonah,* and *wind*.

Practice reading your labels to someone in your home.

### Fluency Check

Set the timer for one minute and see how many words in the passage you can read correctly. You are a Mighty Reader!

# Joseph and the Colorful Coat

## *Vocabulary*

The list of words below will be in the story. Take a few minutes to discuss the meanings of these words with your child before beginning to read. Ask your child to repeat them to you and use them in a sentence.

**special:** something that is your favorite

**colorful:** being full of color

**tricked:** were sneaky, caused confusion

**leader:** someone in charge

**forgave:** showed forgiveness

Biblical terms: Jacob, Joseph, Egypt, Pharaoh

## *Skills*

Refer to the Reading Skills Guide on page 7 for a detailed explanation about many of these skills.

Context Clues

Main Character

Key Details

Setting

Problem/Solution

Synonyms

Connecting Writing with Reading

Text Feature—Labels

Vocabulary

# Joseph and the Colorful Coat

*from Genesis 37; 39; 41–47*

1. There was a man named Jacob. His special son was Joseph. He loved Joseph very much. Joseph's brothers were mad.

2. Jacob gave Joseph a colorful coat. Joseph loved his new coat. This made his brothers angry.

3. The brothers tricked and sold Joseph. They told a lie to their father and said Joseph had died. Jacob was very sad.

4. Joseph was taken to jail in Egypt. Pharaoh was the king. Joseph understood dreams. He even helped Pharaoh with his dreams. This made Pharaoh happy. He made Joseph a leader in Egypt.

5. Later, Joseph's brothers came to Egypt. He gave them food. He also forgave them. He said God took something bad to make something good. Joseph's family came to Egypt too.

6. God was always with Joseph. He even gave Joseph back his family. Sometimes bad things happen, but God can work through them!

God will always be with you, Mighty Reader.

25

# Day 1

**1** Read the story as an *echo read* with someone in your home.

**2** Reread paragraph 1. Who was Jacob's special son? Underline evidence in yellow to show where you found your answer. Write your answer in the box.

(empty box)

**3** What do you think the word **special** means? Circle the word in blue in the text. Write your answer in the box.

(empty box)

**4** What does the word **leader** mean in the following sentence? *He made Joseph a leader in Egypt.* Write your answer in the box.

(empty box)

# Day 2

## Skills: Key Details, Cause/Effect

**1** Read the story as a *choral read* with someone in your home.

**2** Reread paragraph 2. What caused Joseph to be tricked and sold? Write it in the box.

**3** Reread paragraph 4. How did all the bad things affect Joseph? Write the effect in the box.

**4** Who is the main character of the story? Find his name in the text and circle it in (green). Write his name in the box.

# Day 3

*Skills: Key Details, Inferencing, Visualization*

1. Read the story as a *cloze read* with someone in your home.

2. Reread paragraph 2. What caused Joseph's brothers to become angry? Write it in the box.

3. What does the word **tricked** mean?

   O were sneaky
   O were fair
   O were kind

4. Who was the king of Egypt? Write his name in the box.

# Day 4

1. Read the story as a *partner read* with someone in your home.

2. What do you think **colorful** means in the following sentence? *Jacob gave Joseph a colorful coat.* Write your answer in the box.

    ┌─────────────────────────────────────┐
    │                                     │
    │                                     │
    │                                     │
    │                                     │
    └─────────────────────────────────────┘

3. Reread paragraph 4. What is the setting of the story? Write it in the box.

    ┌─────────────────────────────────────┐
    │                                     │
    │                                     │
    │                                     │
    │                                     │
    └─────────────────────────────────────┘

4. Reread paragraph 5. What <u>two</u> things did Joseph give his brothers? Write your answers in the box.

    ┌─────────────────────────────────────┐
    │                                     │
    │                                     │
    │                                     │
    └─────────────────────────────────────┘

# Day 5

1 Read the story as an *independent reader* to someone in your home. Ask someone for help if you get stuck on a word.

2 Respond to the reading through *writing*. Don't forget to use the correct punctuation in your sentences, and try to add some detail words too. Try your best!

Joseph received a colorful coat from his father. Write about something else you know that is colorful. Name the item and describe what it looks like.

_____

_____

_____

_____

_____

_____

_____

Make it your goal to write at least three sentences. After you finish your sentences, read them aloud to someone in your home.

# Day 6

Use your writing tools to *draw and color a picture* of Joseph's colorful coat. After drawing your picture, write a *caption* under your illustration describing the coat.

Write your caption in the box below.

### *Fluency Check*

Set the timer for one minute and see how many words in the passage you can read correctly. You are a Mighty Reader!

# Moses and the Ten Plagues

## *Vocabulary*

The list of words below will be in the story. Take a few minutes to discuss the meanings of these words with your child before beginning to read. Ask your child to repeat them to you and use them in a sentence.

**series:** things happening in a certain order

**plague:** trouble

**livestock:** cattle

**boils:** sores

**swarm:** a large group

**hail:** frozen rain

**Biblical terms: Moses, Egypt, Pharaoh**

## *Skills*

Refer to the Reading Skills Guide on page 7 for a detailed explanation about many of these skills.

| | |
|---|---|
| Key Details | Visualization |
| Context Clues | Connecting Writing with Reading |
| Sequencing | Text Features—Labels |
| Repetition | Vocabulary |

# Moses and the Ten Plagues

*from Genesis 7–11; 12:29–32*

1 There was a man named **Moses**. He went to **Egypt**. God sent him to talk to **Pharaoh**. God wanted the Hebrew slaves set free. Pharaoh said, "No." God sent a **series** of plagues.

2 First, God turned the water to blood. Second, He sent an army of frogs. Third, He sent a **plague** of itchy lice. Fourth, flies were scattered everywhere. Pharaoh still said, "No."

3 The **livestock** died during the fifth plague. The sixth covered people with **boils**. The seventh plague poured down large balls of **hail**. Pharaoh still said, "No."

4 The eighth plague was a **swarm** of locusts. The ninth caused darkness for three days. The final plague killed all of the first-born children. Pharaoh's son died. Pharaoh was sad.

5 He finally let the people go. Moses and his people left Egypt. God is powerful! He gave Moses courage. He can give you courage.

Do not be afraid, Mighty Reader!

# Day 1

*Skills: Key Details, Context Clues*

**1** Read the story as an *echo read* with someone in your home.

**2** Reread paragraph 1. What did Moses talk to Pharaoh about? Write your answer in the box below. Underline evidence in the text in yellow to show where you found your answer.

**3** What do you think the word **livestock** means in paragraph 3? Write your answer in the box.

**4** What does the word **swarm** mean in the following sentence? *The eighth plague was a swarm of locusts.* Write your answer in the box.

# Day 2

*Skills: Sequencing, Key Details, Context Clues*

1   Read the story as a *choral read* with someone in your home.

2   Reread paragraph 2. Sequence the plagues in order as you read the paragraph. Write your answers in the boxes.

| | | | |
|---|---|---|---|
| | | | |

3   Reread paragraph 4. Which plague caused darkness for three days? Write your answer in the box.

4   Circle the **bold print** word in (green) that means "things happening in a certain order." Write the word in the box below.

# Day 3

## *Skills: Sequencing, Repetition, Visualization*

1. Read the story as a *cloze read* with someone in your home.

2. Reread paragraph 3. Sequence the plagues in order as you read the paragraph. Write your answers in the boxes.

| | | |
|---|---|---|
| | | |

3. There is some evidence of repetition, words that are repeated, in paragraphs 2 and 3. Circle the sentences that are repeated in (blue).

4. Reread paragraph 3 and circle the word **hail** in (blue). Draw a picture of hail pouring down from the sky in the box.

# Day 4

1 Read the story as a *partner read* with someone in your home.

2 Reread paragraph 5. Fill in the missing words from the following sentences:

He finally let the _____ go. Moses and his people

left _____.

3 Reread paragraph 4. Sequence the plagues in order as you read the paragraph. Write your answers in the boxes.

| | | |
|---|---|---|
| | | |

4 Reread paragraph 2. How did the plague of lice make the people feel? Circle your answer in (blue) and write it in the box.

| |
|---|
| |

# Day 5

1. Read the story as an *independent reader* to someone in your home. Ask someone for help if you get stuck on a word.

2. Respond to the reading through *writing*. Make it your goal to write at least 3 sentences. Don't forget to use the correct punctuation in your sentences and try to add some detail words too. Give it your very best!

3. On the lines below, write about what you think it would have been like to experience a plague of frogs. After you finish your sentences, read them aloud to someone in your home.

# Day 6

*Skills: Illustrations and Comprehension, Text Features*

Use your writing tools to *draw and color a picture* of the ninth plague: darkness. After drawing your picture, *label* different parts of your picture. You can include and label things such as a black sky, trees, grass, houses, and people.

Practice reading your labels to someone in your home. How do you think the people felt during those three dark days?

### Fluency Check

Set the timer for one minute, and see how many words in the passage you can read correctly. You are a Mighty Reader!

# David and Goliath

## *Vocabulary*

The list of words below will be in the story. Take a few minutes to discuss the meanings of these words with your child before beginning to read. Ask your child to repeat them to you and use them in a sentence.

**shepherd:** someone who takes care of sheep

**giant:** a very tall person

**army:** a group of soldiers

**sling:** a leather strap with a pouch

**crashed:** fell down

Biblical terms: **David, Goliath**

## *Skills*

Refer to the Reading Skills Guide on page 7 for a detailed explanation about many of these skills.

| | |
|---|---|
| Key Details | Multiple Meanings |
| Root Words | Repetition |
| Context Clues | Connecting Writing with Reading |
| Sequencing | Text Features—Captions |
| Phonics | Vocabulary |

# David and Goliath

*from 1 Samuel 17:1–51*

1. There was a boy named **David**. He took care of sheep. He was a **shepherd**. He was brave.

2. **Goliath** was a big, strong **giant**. He was almost ten feet tall! Goliath fought with a powerful **army**. Everyone was scared of Goliath, but not David. God chose David to fight Goliath.

3. David trusted God. His sheep were kept safe by God. God would keep David safe when he fought Goliath too.

4. David brought a **sling** and five stones. Goliath laughed at him. Goliath was strong, but God was stronger.

5. David ran at Goliath. David put a stone in his sling. The sling went around, and around, and around. The stone flew in the air and hit Goliath in the head.

6. The giant **crashed** to the ground. Boom, boom, boom. God had helped a shepherd boy kill the giant! Now the army was scared, so they ran away.

7. David trusted God. God kept David safe. God keeps you safe too. When you feel scared, God will keep you safe.

**Do not be afraid, Mighty Reader! Trust God as David did.**

# Day 1

## *Skills: Key Details, Root Words, Context Clues*

1 Read the story as an *echo read* with someone in your home.

2 Reread paragraph 2. What did God choose David for? Underline evidence in <u>yellow</u> to show where you found your answer. Write your answer in the box.

3 Circle the word crashed in (blue) in the text. What is the root word or hidden word in crashed? Write it in the box.

4 What does the word giant mean in the following sentence? *He was a big, strong giant.* Write your answer in the box.

# Day 2

*Skills: Sequencing (Beginning, Middle, End)*

1 Read the story as a *choral read* with someone in your home.

2 Reread paragraph 1. What did David take care of at the *beginning* of the story? Write your answer in the box.

```

```

3 Reread paragraph 4, the *middle* of the story. What weapons did David use to fight Goliath? Write your answers in the boxes.

| | |
|---|---|
| | |

4 Reread paragraph 6. What happened to the giant at the *end* of the story? Write your answer in the box.

```

```

# Day 3

*Skills: Phonics, Multiple Meanings, Repetition*

1 Read the story as a *cloze read* with someone in your home.

2 Reread paragraph 1. David was a **shepherd**. Write the word **shepherd** neatly in the box. Circle the vowels in (yellow) and put an orange ● under all the consonants in the word.

```



```

3 What does the word **sling** mean in this story?

O To throw something
O A weapon in the shape of a strap
O A strap used to support something

4 Reread paragraphs 5 and 6. Look for *repetition*. What words are repeated in these paragraphs? Circle the words in (blue). Write the words in the box.

```



```

# Day 4

## Skills: Repetition, Key Details

1 Read the story as a *partner read* with someone in your home.

2 Reread paragraph 6. Look for *sound words*. Write the words in the box.

3 Reread paragraph 3. How did God help David before he fought Goliath? Write your answer in the box.

4 Reread paragraph 6. How did the army feel after David killed Goliath? Underline evidence in <u>yellow</u> and write your answer in the box.

# Day 5

1 Read the story as an *independent reader* to someone in your home. Ask someone for help if you get stuck on a word.

2 Respond to the reading through *writing*. Don't forget to use the correct punctuation in your sentences, and try to add some detail words too. You will do great!

On the lines below, write answers to the following questions: How did David beat Goliath? What things did David need to beat Goliath?

_____

_____

_____

_____

_____

_____

_____

Make it your goal to write at least three sentences. After you finish your sentences, read them aloud to someone in your home.

# Day 6

Use your writing tools to *draw and color a picture* of a shepherd taking care of his sheep. After drawing your picture, write a *caption* under your illustration that talks about David taking care of his sheep.

Write your caption in the box below.

*Fluency Check*

Set the timer for one minute, and see how many words in the passage you can read correctly. You are a Mighty Reader!

# Three Friends in a Fiery Furnace

## *Vocabulary*

The list of words below will be in the story. Take a few minutes to discuss the meanings of these words with your child before beginning to read. Ask your child to repeat them to you and use them in a sentence.

**statue:** a large figure made of concrete or other material

**bow down:** to bend down and show respect

**worship:** to show honor to something

**fiery:** filled with or burning with fire

**furnace:** a hot stove

**rescue:** to save

**faith:** belief in something unseen

Biblical terms: **King Nebuchadnezzar, Shadrach, Meshach, Abednego**

## *Skills*

Refer to the Reading Skills Guide on page 7 for a detailed explanation about many of these skills.

| | |
|---|---|
| Determining the Lesson | Synonyms |
| Problem/Solution | Visualization |
| Context Clues | Connecting Writing with Reading |
| Key Details | Text Features—Labels |
| Phonics | Vocabulary |

# Three Friends in a Fiery Furnace

*from Daniel 3:1–4:3*

1 King Nebuchadnezzar (neb uh kuhd NEZ uhr) lived long ago. He was a mean king. He made a tall, gold statue. He wanted everyone to bow down to it. He said they had to worship the statue when they heard music.

2 The king made a rule. Anyone who did not worship the statue would be punished. They would be thrown in a fiery furnace. This made the people afraid!

3 Three men were not afraid. They trusted in God. Their names were Shadrach, Meshach, and Abednego. The king brought the men to him. He asked them to bow down, but they said, "No." They only bowed down to God.

4 The men were thrown in the fiery furnace. They were not afraid. They said God would rescue them. God sent an angel to be with them in the furnace. The men did not get burned! The king was shocked. He believed in God after seeing this miracle.

5 God cared for Shadrach, Meshach, and Abednego. Their faith made them strong. They took a stand for their faith even when there was danger.

**Always stay strong in your faith. God will be pleased, Mighty Reader!**

# Day 1

**1** Read the story as an *echo read* with someone in your home.

**2** Reread paragraph 5. What lesson can you learn from the story? Underline evidence in the text in <u>yellow</u> to show where you found your answer.

[ ]

**3** What is the *problem* in paragraph 2? Write it in the box.

[ ]

**4** What is the *solution* in paragraph 4? Write it in the box.

[ ]

50

# Day 2

*Skills: Key Details, Context Clues*

**1** Read the story as a *choral read* with someone in your home.

**2** Reread paragraph 4. What were <u>three</u> major events that happened in this story? Write them in the boxes.

| |
|---|
| 1. |
| 2. |
| 3. |

**3** Reread paragraph 3. What word would you use to describe the characters Shadrach, Meshach, and Abednego? Underline evidence in <u>yellow</u> that helped you think in this way.

| |
|---|
| |

**4** Circle the word in (green) that means "filled with fire." Write the word in the box below.

| |
|---|
| |

# Day 3

*Skills: Phonics, Synonyms*

1  Read the story as a *cloze read* with someone in your home.

2  Reread paragraph 1. Circle the words **bow down** in (blue). Write the words in the box. Circle in (blue) the letters in the words that make the same sound.

 

3  Reread paragraph 4. Circle the word **rescue** in (orange). What is a synonym or word that means the same thing as **rescue**? Write it in the box.

 

4  God is pleased when we have faith in Him. Write the word **faith** neatly in the box below. Trace the vowels in **orange** and the consonants in **blue**.

 

# Day 4

*Skills: Context Clues*

**1** Read the story as a *partner read* with someone in your home.

**2** Reread paragraph 5. Fill in the missing words from the following sentence:

They took a _____ for their _____

even when there was _____.

**3** Reread paragraph 4. Who kept the three men safe in the fiery furnace? Write your answer in the box.

<br><br><br><br><br><br><br><br>

**4** Reread paragraph 1. Circle the word **worship** in (blue). What do you think the word **worship** means?

<br><br><br><br><br><br><br>

# Day 5

*Skills: Connecting Writing with Reading*

1 Read the story as an *independent reader* to someone in your home. Ask someone for help if you get stuck on a word.

2 Respond to the reading through *writing*. Don't forget to use the correct punctuation in your sentences, and try to add some detail words too. You're an awesome writer!

On the lines below, write about how Shadrach, Meshach, and Abednego showed faith and courage.

_____

_____

_____

_____

_____

_____

_____

_____

Make it your goal to write at least three sentences. After you finish your sentences, read them aloud to someone in your home.

# Day 6

Use your writing tools to *draw and color a picture* of the fiery furnace with the three men and the angel. After drawing your picture, *label* different parts of your picture. Include labels such as *furnace, fiery, men, angel,* and *king.*

Practice reading your labels to someone in your home.

## *Fluency Check*

Set the timer for one minute and see how many words in the passage you can read correctly. You are a Mighty Reader!

# Daniel and the Lions

## *Vocabulary*

The list of words below will be in the story. Take a few minutes to discuss the meanings of these words with your child before beginning to read. Ask your child to repeat them to you and use them in a sentence.

**officials:** people who were in charge

**favorite:** something that is special

**trustworthy:** someone or something you can trust

**law:** a set of rules

**den:** an animal home; cave

**protect:** to keep safe

Biblical terms: **King Darius, Daniel**

## *Skills*

Refer to the Reading Skills Guide on page 7 for a detailed explanation about many of these skills.

Key Details

Adjectives

Context Clues

Compound Words

Visualization

Inferencing

Connecting Writing with Reading

Text Features—Headings

Vocabulary

# Daniel and the Lions

### from Daniel 6

1. There was a ruler named **King Darius**. He had many **officials**. They were people who were in charge. His **favorite** official was **Daniel**. This made the other officials mad.

2. Daniel was a great official. He was **trustworthy**. Daniel loved God. He also loved to pray.

3. The other officials did not like Daniel. They had King Darius make a new **law**. It said that people had to pray to King Darius. Those who broke the law would be put into a **den** of lions.

4. Daniel still prayed to God. The officials told King Darius. Daniel was put into the den of lions. They were happy that Daniel got caught. The king was sad and worried.

5. The next morning, the king ran to the den. Daniel was safe! God sent an angel to **protect** him. The angel shut the mouths of the lions! The king made a new law. It said that all people must fear Daniel's God.

6. God was with Daniel at a scary time. He will be with you at scary times too.

When you feel scared, pray to God. Mighty Reader, He always hears your prayers!

# Day 1

1  Read the story as an *echo read* with someone in your home.

2  Reread paragraph 1. Who was King Darius's **favorite** official? Circle his name in (green). Write your answer in the box.

[                                                                    ]

3  Reread paragraph 2. In the box, write two words (adjectives) that would describe Daniel.

[                                                                    ]

4  What does the word **den** mean in the following sentence? *Those who disobeyed would be put into a **den** of lions.* Write your answer in the box.

[                                                                    ]

# Day 2

*Skills: Compound Words, Key Details, Context Clues*

**1** Read the story as a *choral read* with someone in your home.

**2** Reread paragraph 2. Circle the compound word in (green). What two words make this compound word? Write them in the boxes.

|  |  |
|---|---|
|  |  |

**3** Who are two main characters in this story? Write their names in the boxes. Remember to reread.

|  |  |
|---|---|
|  |  |

**4** What does the word **protect** mean in the following sentence? *God sent an angel to protect* him. Write your answer in the box.

|  |
|---|
|  |

# Day 3

*Skills: Key Details, Context Clues, Visualization*

1. Read the story as a *cloze read* with someone in your home.

2. Reread paragraph 4. How did the officials feel when Daniel got caught? Underline evidence in yellow. Write it in the box.

3. What does the word law mean?

   O An idea
   O A rule
   O A question

4. Read this sentence: *God sent an angel to protect him.* Draw an angel in the box below.

# Day 4

*Skills: Context Clues, Adjectives, Inferencing*

1 Read the story as a *partner read* with someone in your home.

2 Reread paragraph 1. What does the word **officials** mean? Underline text evidence in <u>yellow</u>. Write your answer in the box.

[ ]

3 Reread paragraph 4. What kind of word would you use to describe the other officials? Write it in the box.

[ ]

4 Reread paragraph 5. What do you think it means when the text says "the angel shut the mouths of the lions"?

[ ]

# Day 5

*Skills: Connecting Writing with Reading*

1  Read the story as an *independent reader* to someone in your home. Ask someone for help if you get stuck on a word.

2  Respond to the reading through *writing*. Don't forget to use the correct punctuation in your sentences, and try to add some detail words too. You can do it!

Think about Daniel sitting in the den with the lions. Write about what it might have looked like inside the den.

_____

_____

_____

_____

_____

_____

_____

_____

Make it your goal to write at least three sentences. After you finish your sentences, read them aloud to someone in your home.

# Day 6

*Skills: Illustrations and Comprehension, Text Features*

Use your writing tools to *draw and color a picture* of Daniel and the lions' den in the large box below. After drawing your picture, write a *heading* in the box above your illustration. (A heading is at the top of a page and gives the reader information about the text or an illustration.)

*Fluency Check*

Set the timer for one minute and see how many words in the passage you can read correctly. You are a Mighty Reader!

# Queen Esther

## *Vocabulary*

The list of words below will be in the story. Take a few minutes to discuss the meanings of these words with your child before beginning to read. Ask your child to repeat them to you and use them in a sentence.

**admired:** delighted in

**servant:** a helper

**rage:** strong anger

**risky:** possibly dangerous

**banquet:** a formal evening meal

**desired:** wanted something

**Biblical terms:** Esther, Jew, Mordecai, king of Babylon, Haman

## *Skills*

Refer to the Reading Skills Guide on page 7 for a detailed explanation about many of these skills.

| | |
|---|---|
| Key Details | Visualization |
| Context Clues | Connecting Writing with Reading |
| Adjectives | Text Features—Headings |
| Root Words | Vocabulary |

# Queen Esther

### *from Esther 2–7*

1. There lived a woman named **Esther**. She was a **Jew**. She was very beautiful. She had a Jewish uncle named **Mordecai** (MOR deh ky). He was a special part of her life.

2. One day, the **king of Babylon** wanted a new queen. Many women came to see him. The king chose Esther. He **admired** her beauty. He did not know she was a Jew.

3. **Haman** was the king's **servant**. He did not like Jews. He made the Jews bow down to him. Mordecai would not bow down. This filled Haman with **rage**. He began to make a plan to kill the Jews.

4. Queen Esther had an idea. She knew it was **risky**. She made a request to the king. She invited the king and Haman to a **banquet**. The king agreed, and he enjoyed the banquet.

5. The king told Esther he would give her whatever she **desired**. She asked the king to save the Jews! The king told Esther that the Jews would not be harmed. Haman was taken away, and the Jews were safe!

6. God was with Esther! He gave her courage to do what was right.

**God will help you make the right choices too, Mighty Reader!**

# Day 1

## *Skills: Key Details, Context Clues*

1. Read the story as an *echo read* with someone in your home.

2. Reread paragraph 2. Who did the king of Babylon choose to be his next queen? Write your answer in the box.

   [ ]

3. Reread this sentence: *This filled Haman with rage!* What do you think the word **rage** means in this sentence? Write your answer in the box.

   [ ]

4. Which character from the story did not like Jews? Underline evidence in <u>yellow</u> that helped you know your answer. Write your answer in the box.

   [ ]

# Day 2

*Skills: Key Details, Context Clues*

**1** Read the story as a *choral read* with someone in your home.

**2** Reread paragraph 1. Who was a special part of Esther's life? Write your answer in the box.

> (blank box)

**3** Reread paragraph 2. What did the king not know about Esther? Underline text evidence in yellow. Write your answer in the box.

> (blank box)

**4** Reread paragraph 4. Circle the word in (red) that means a "fancy dinner." Write the word in the box below.

> (blank box)

# Day 3

*Skills: Key Details, Adjectives, Root Words*

**1** Read the story as a *cloze read* with someone in your home.

**2** Reread paragraph 5. What did Queen Esther ask of the king? Underline evidence in yellow. Write your answer in the box.

```
[                                                        ]
```

**3** Reread paragraph 1. What is an adjective, a describing word, that describes Queen Esther? Write your answer in the box.

```
[                                                        ]
```

**4** Circle the word **risky** in (green). This word means that bad things could have happened to Queen Esther. What is the root word in **risky**? Write your answer in the box.

```
[                                                        ]
```

# Day 4

*Skills: Context Clues, Key Details*

**1** Read the story as a *partner read* with someone in your home.

**2** Reread paragraph 5. Fill in the missing words from the following sentence:

The king told _____ that the _____ would not be harmed.

**3** Reread this sentence: *The king told Esther he would give her whatever she desired.* What is another word that means the same thing as **desired**? Write your answer in the box.

[ ]

**4** Reread paragraph 3. Who was the king's servant? Circle the name in (green). Write your answer in the box.

[ ]

# Day 5

*Skills: Connecting Writing with Reading*

1. Read the story as an *independent reader* to someone in your home. Ask someone for help if you get stuck on a word.

2. Respond to the reading through *writing*. Don't forget to use the correct punctuation in your sentences and try to add some detail words too. Give it your very best!

Queen Esther invited the king and Haman to a banquet. Write below about a time you were invited to a special event. What did you celebrate? What did you do? What did you eat?

_____

_____

_____

_____

_____

_____

_____

_____

Make it your goal to write at least three sentences. After you finish your sentences, read them aloud to someone in your home.

# Day 6

*Skills: Illustrations and Comprehension, Text Features*

Use your writing tools to *draw and color a picture* in the large box of how Queen Esther's crown might have looked. Be sure to include details on your crown. Then write a *heading* that describes your crown in the rectangle above the picture box.

Practice reading your *heading* to someone in your home.

### Fluency Check

Set the timer for one minute, and see how many words in the passage you can read correctly. You are a Mighty Reader!

# Jesus Is Born

## *Vocabulary*

The list of words below will be in the story. Take a few minutes to discuss the meanings of these words with your child before beginning to read. Ask your child to repeat them to you and use them in a sentence.

**carpenter:** a person who works with wood

**journey:** a long trip

**stable:** a place where animals are kept

**manger:** a place to feed animals hay

**wise men:** men who studied stars

Biblical terms: **Mary**, **Jesus**, **Joseph**, **Bethlehem**, **Savior**

## *Skills*

Refer to the Reading Skills Guide on page 7 for a detailed explanation about many of these skills.

Key Details

Context Clues

Problem/Solution

Sequencing

Setting

Visualization

Connecting Writing with Reading

Text Features—Labels

Vocabulary

# Jesus Is Born

*from Matthew 1:18—2:11; Luke 2:1–7*

1. There was a young lady named **Mary**. She was chosen by God. He sent an angel to visit her. The angel told Mary she would have a baby boy. His name would be **Jesus**. He would be the Son of God.

2. Mary was going to marry **Joseph**. He was a **carpenter**. They traveled to **Bethlehem**. It was a long and hard **journey**. When they arrived, there was no place for them to stay.

3. Mary and Joseph had to sleep in a **stable**. There were animals too. Soon Jesus was born. He was wrapped in cloth. Mary placed Jesus in a **manger**. God's Son had come to the world!

4. An angel visited some shepherds nearby. They were taking care of sheep. The angel told them a **Savior** was born. They were so happy! They went to see Jesus.

5. Some **wise men** also came to visit. They saw a new star in the sky. They followed the star to find the new King. They brought Him gifts. They kneeled and worshiped Jesus. They were excited to meet the new King!

6. God chose Mary. He will choose you to do great things too.

Remember to share the good news, Mighty Reader. Jesus is the King!

Good news!

# Day 1

## *Skills: Key Details, Context Clues*

1. Read the story as an *echo read* with someone in your home.

2. Reread paragraph 1. Who did God send to tell Mary a message? Write your answer in the box below. Underline evidence in the text in yellow to show where you found your answer.

3. Find the word **stable** in the text. What do you think the word **stable** means? Write it in the box.

4. What is the name of the man who Mary was going to marry? Write it in the box.

# Day 2

*Skills: Key Details, Problem/Solution*

1. Read the story as a *choral read* with someone in your home.

2. Reread paragraph 2. Where did Mary and Joseph travel to? Write your answer in the box.

3. Reread paragraph 2. What is the *problem* in paragraph 2? Write it in the box. Underline evidence in <u>blue</u>.

4. Reread paragraph 3. What is the *solution* in paragraph 3? Write it in the box. Underline evidence in <u>green</u>.

# Day 3

*Skills: Sequencing, Setting*

1. Read the story as a *cloze read* with someone in your home.

2. Reread paragraph 4. Who came to visit baby Jesus *first*? Write your answer in the box.

3. Reread paragraph 5. Who came to visit baby Jesus *last*? Write your answer in the box.

4. Reread paragraph 3. What is the *setting* in paragraph 3? Underline evidence in yellow. Write your answer in the box.

# Day 4

*Skills: Key Details*

1. Read the story as a *partner read* with someone in your home.

2. Reread paragraph 5. What did the wise men see in the sky? Underline evidence in <u>yellow</u>. Write your answer in the box.

```



```

3. What did the wise men bring baby Jesus? Write your answer in the box.

```



```

4. Reread paragraph 4. How did the shepherds feel when they heard a Savior was born? Underline evidence in <u>yellow</u>. Write your answer in the box.

```



```

# Day 5

*Skills: Connecting Writing with Reading*

1 Read the story as an *independent reader* to someone in your home. Ask someone for help if you get stuck on a word.

2 Respond to the reading through *writing*. Don't forget to use the correct punctuation in your sentences, and try to add some detail words too.

On the lines below, write about the stable where Jesus was born. What kinds of animals would you have seen? What sounds would you have heard? What would it have smelled like?

_____

_____

_____

_____

_____

_____

_____

Make it your goal to write at least three sentences. After you finish your sentences, read them aloud to someone in your home. You are an awesome writer!

# Day 6

Use your writing tools to *draw and color a picture* of the stable. Be sure to put a star above it. After drawing your picture, *label* different parts of your picture. Include words such as *stable, star, hay, animals,* and *manger.*

Practice reading your labels to someone in your home.

### *Fluency Check*

Set the timer for one minute, and see how many words in the passage you can read correctly. You are a Mighty Reader!

# Zacchaeus Climbs a Tree

## *Vocabulary*

The list of words below will be in the story. Take a few minutes to discuss the meanings of these words with your child before beginning to read. Ask your child to repeat them to you and use them in a sentence.

**sneaky:** sly; dishonest

**tax collector:** a person who collects unpaid taxes

**sycamore tree:** a type of tree found in the Bible

**view:** to see something

**changed:** became different

**generous:** gives a lot to others

Biblical terms: **Zacchaeus, Jesus**

## *Skills*

Refer to the Reading Skills Guide on page 7 for a detailed explanation about many of these skills.

Key Details                    Visualization

Sequencing                     Connecting Writing with Reading

Phonics                        Text Features—Labels

Synonyms                       Vocabulary

# Zacchaeus Climbs a Tree

*from Luke 19:1–10*

1. There was a short, sneaky man named Zacchaeus. He was a tax collector. He did not have many friends. He cheated people and stole their money.

2. One day Jesus came to town. Zacchaeus wanted to see Him. Zacchaeus could not see over the crowd of people. He was too short. So he climbed up a sycamore tree for a better view.

3. When Jesus passed by, He saw Zacchaeus. He told him to come down from the tree. Jesus wanted to eat with him at his house. Zacchaeus was so excited! He had a new friend.

4. Zacchaeus was forever changed. He told the people he was sorry. He paid back the stolen money. He even gave them extra money. He also helped the poor. He was no longer a thief. He was a generous man.

5. The tax collector did not think anyone liked him, until he met Jesus. He found a true friend. You can be a good friend too.

Love other people like Jesus does, Mighty Reader!

HELLO

# Day 1

*Skills: Character, Key Details, Context Clues*

1. Read the story as an *echo read* with someone in your home.

2. Reread paragraph 1. Who is the main character of this story? Underline evidence in the text in yellow to show where you found your answer.

[ ]

3. Reread paragraph 2. What kind of tree did Zacchaeus climb? Write it in the box.

[ ]

4. What do the words "for a better view" mean at the end of paragraph 2? Write it in the box.

[ ]

# Day 2

*Skills: Key Details, Sequencing*

**1** Read the story as a *choral read* with someone in your home.

**2** What kind of man was Zacchaeus at the beginning of the story? Write your answer in the box.

```




```

**3** Reread paragraphs 3 and 4. Who helped to **change** Zacchaeus? Write your answer in the box.

```




```

**4** What kind of man was Zacchaeus at the end of the story? Write your answer in the box.

```




```

# Day 3

*Skills: Phonics, Synonyms, Key Details*

**1** Read the story as a *cloze read* with someone in your home.

**2** Reread paragraph 1. Circle the words tax collector in (blue). Write the words in the box. Trace the letters that are vowels in yellow and the consonants in orange.

[ ]

**3** Reread paragraph 1. Circle the word sneaky in (green). What is a synonym or word that means the same thing as sneaky? Write it in the box.

[ ]

**4** Reread paragraph 3. How did Zacchaeus feel when Jesus wanted to come to his house? Write your answer in the box.

[ ]

# Day 4

### *Skills: Context Clues, Key Details*

**1** Read the story as a *partner read* with someone in your home.

**2** Reread paragraph 4. Fill in the missing words from the following sentences:

He was no longer a _____. He was a

_____ man.

**3** Zacchaeus became a **generous** man. This meant he gave money to others. Write another sentence with the word **generous** on the lines below.

_____

_____

_____

_____

_____

**4** Reread paragraph 5. How can you be a good friend to others? Write your answer in the box.

```



```

# Day 5

## *Skills: Connecting Writing with Reading*

1 Read the story as an *independent reader* to someone in your home. Ask someone for help if you get stuck on a word.

2 Respond to the reading through *writing*. Don't forget to use the correct punctuation in your sentences and try to add some detail words too. You will do great!

Jesus went to Zacchaeus's house to eat a meal. Write about what you would offer Jesus to eat if He came to your house for lunch. What would you talk to Him about?

_____

_____

_____

_____

_____

_____

_____

Make it your goal to write at least three sentences. After you finish your sentences, read them aloud to someone in your home.

# Day 6

## Skills: Illustrations and Comprehension, Text Features

Use your writing tools to *draw and color a picture* of Zacchaeus up in a sycamore tree. After drawing your picture, *label* different parts of your picture. Include labels such as *leaves*, *trunk*, *branches*, *sycamore tree*, and *Zacchaeus*.

Practice reading your labels to someone in your home.

### Fluency Check

Set the timer for one minute, and see how many words in the passage you can read correctly. You are a Mighty Reader!

# Jesus Feeds the 5,000

## *Vocabulary*

The list of words below will be in the story. Take a few minutes to discuss the meanings of these words with your child before beginning to read. Ask your child to repeat them to you and use them in a sentence.

**miracles:** amazing things God does

**grin:** a smile

**feast:** a very large meal

**bread of life:** a spiritual fullness

**invited:** asked to do something

**provider:** someone who gives you what you need

Biblical terms: **Jesus, disciples**

## *Skills*

Refer to the Reading Skills Guide on page 7 for a detailed explanation about many of these skills.

| | |
|---|---|
| Context Clues | Sequencing |
| Inferencing | Phonics |
| Key Details | Connecting Writing with Reading |
| Drawing Conclusions | Text Features—Captions |
| Visualization | Vocabulary |

# Jesus Feeds the 5,000

### from John 6:1–14, 22–40

1. People began to follow **Jesus**. He did a lot of **miracles**, or amazing events. People wanted to see and be a part of the miracles. They came to listen to and watch Jesus.

2. One day there were more than 5,000 people around Jesus. They were hungry. They needed a lot of food. A boy gave up his small lunch. It had two fish and five loaves of bread.

3. The people felt there wasn't enough food. Jesus did not feel the same. The **disciples** grouped the people. Jesus gave a **grin**. He held the fish and bread.

4. Jesus thanked God for the food. Then He began to give it to the people. The disciples helped Him. The people shared with each other.

5. There was a lot of food! It was like a **feast**! There was even extra food. Jesus told the people, "I am the **bread of life!**"

6. He **invited** the people to believe in Him. He told them He would take care of their needs.

**Jesus is a provider. He will give you what you need too, Mighty Reader!**

# Day 1

*Skills: Key Details, Context Clues, Visualization*

1 Read the story as an *echo read* with someone in your home.

2 Reread paragraph 2. How many people did Jesus feed? Underline evidence in yellow to show where you found your answer. Write your answer in the box.

3 Reread paragraph 1. What is a **miracle**? Underline evidence in red. Write your answer in the box.

4 ⬭Circle the word **grin** in the text. Draw a face with a grin in the box below.

# Day 2

*Skills: Drawing Conclusions, Sequencing, Context Clues*

1  Read the story as a *choral read* with someone in your home.

2  Reread paragraph 3. How did the people feel about the boy's lunch? Write it in the box.

[ ]

3  Reread paragraph 4. What did Jesus do before He passed out food to the people? Underline evidence in yellow. Write it in the box.

[ ]

4  Circle the word in (red) that means "a lot of food." Write it in the box.

[ ]

# Day 3

*Skills: Key Details, Phonics, Context Clues*

1. Read the story as a *cloze read* with someone in your home.

2. The text says, "I am the **bread of life**." This means we will feel full or satisfied when Jesus lives in us. Write the name *Jesus* in the box. Trace the vowels in **orange** and the consonants in **blue**.

```




```

3. What does the word **invited** mean?

   O  To be asked to do something
   O  To be told to stay away
   O  To be left alone

4. (Circle) the word **provider** in the text. This word means someone who gives you what you need. How did Jesus provide for the 5,000? Finish the sentence below.

   Jesus provided for the 5,000 by _____

   _____.

# Day 4

*Skills: Key Details*

**1**  Read the story as a *partner read* with someone in your home.

**2**  Reread paragraph 1. What did the people like to see Jesus do? Write your answer in the box.

<br>

**3**  Reread paragraph 2. What was in the boy's lunch? Underline evidence in <u>yellow</u>. Fill in the missing words below.

_____ fish and _____ loaves of bread

**4**  Reread paragraph 3. How did the disciples gather the people? Underline evidence in <u>green</u>. Write your answer in the box.

# Day 5

## *Skills: Connecting Writing with Reading*

1 Read the story as an *independent reader* to someone in your home. Ask someone for help if you get stuck on a word.

2 Respond to the reading through *writing*. Don't forget to use the correct punctuation in your sentences, and try to add some detail words too. Good readers make good writers!

Jesus provided the people with a feast. Write about a Thanksgiving feast you have eaten. What did you eat? Who was with you? Did you eat leftovers the next day?

_____

_____

_____

_____

_____

_____

_____

_____

Make it your goal to write at least three sentences. After you finish your sentences, read them aloud to someone in your home.

# Day 6

*Skills: Illustrations and Comprehension, Text Features*

Use your writing tools to *draw and color a picture* of the boy's lunch that Jesus used to do a miracle. After drawing your picture, write a *caption* under your illustration.

Write your caption in the box below.

*Fluency Check*

Set the timer for one minute, and see how many words in the passage you can read correctly. You are a Mighty Reader!

# Jesus and the Cross

## *Vocabulary*

The list of words below will be in the story. Take a few minutes to discuss the meanings of these words with your child before beginning to read. Ask your child to repeat them to you and use them in a sentence.

**followers:** people who loved Jesus

**remember:** think of

**confused:** unclear, not understanding

**betrayed:** gave away private information about someone

**tomb:** a room carved out of rock

**sealed:** closed tightly

Biblical terms: **Jesus, last supper, Judas, heaven**

## *Skills*

Refer to the Reading Skills Guide on page 7 for a detailed explanation about many of these skills.

| | |
|---|---|
| Key Details | Connecting Writing with Reading |
| Context Clues | Determining the Lesson |
| Sequencing | Text Features—Captions |
| Phonics | Vocabulary |
| Inferencing | |

# Jesus and the Cross

*from Luke 22:1–6, 14–22, 47–48; 23:26–56*

1. **Jesus** had many **followers**. However, some people did not like Him. In fact, some wanted Him to die. Jesus decided to pray. He felt sad. Jesus knew He would be taken to the cross.

2. He shared one **last supper** with His friends. Jesus gave them wine and bread at the supper. These were symbols of His sacrifice. Jesus told His friends to always **remember** Him.

3. His friends felt **confused**. They didn't understand Jesus' words. Later, one of Jesus' friends **betrayed** Him. His name was **Judas**. He told the soldiers where to find Jesus. They came and took Jesus away.

4. Jesus had to carry a heavy cross. Later, He was nailed to that cross. It was very sad. His mother, Mary, stood close by. She was sad too. Soon it was dark outside. Jesus cried out to God one last time.

5. After Jesus died, His body was wrapped in cloth. He was taken to a **tomb**. A heavy stone **sealed** it shut. A soldier stood by to guard the tomb.

6. Jesus died on the cross for our sins. He wanted us to be able to go to **heaven** someday. This sad story is not over yet! Get ready for a happy ending in next week's reading passage!

## Jesus loves you, Mighty Reader!

97

# Day 1

*Skills: Key Details, Context Clues*

1  Read the story as an *echo read* with someone in your home.

2  Reread paragraph 1. What were the people called who loved Jesus? Underline evidence in <u>yellow</u> to show where you found your answer. Write your answer in the box.

3  Why was Jesus sad in paragraph 1? Underline evidence in <u>blue</u>. Write your answer in the box.

4  What does the word sealed mean in the following sentence? *A heavy stone sealed it shut.* Write your answer in the box.

# Day 2

*Skills: Sequencing, Key Details*

1  Read the story as a *choral read* with someone in your home.

2  Reread paragraph 1. How did Jesus feel at the *beginning* of the story? Write your answer in the box.

┌─────────────────────────────────────────────┐
│                                               │
│                                               │
│                                               │
│                                               │
│                                               │
└─────────────────────────────────────────────┘

3  Reread paragraph 2. What two things were symbols of Jesus' sacrifice on the cross? Write your answers in the boxes.

┌──────────────────────┬──────────────────────┐
│ 1.                   │ 2.                   │
│                      │                      │
│                      │                      │
│                      │                      │
└──────────────────────┴──────────────────────┘

4  Reread paragraph 5. Where was Jesus taken after He died on the cross? Underline evidence in yellow. Write your answer in the box.

┌─────────────────────────────────────────────┐
│                                               │
│                                               │
│                                               │
│                                               │
│                                               │
└─────────────────────────────────────────────┘

# Day 3

*Skills: Key Details, Context Clues, Inferencing*

1 Read the story as a *cloze read* with someone in your home.

2 Reread paragraph 3. How did Jesus' friends feel at the last supper? Underline evidence in <u>orange</u>. Write your answer in the box.

3 What does the word **confused** mean?

O clear, understanding
O scared
O unclear, not understanding

4 Reread paragraph 4. Why do you think Mary stood close by Jesus when He was on the cross? Write your answer in the box.

# Day 4

1. Read the story as a *partner read* with someone in your home.

2. Reread paragraph 3. Which of Jesus' friends betrayed Him? Underline evidence in <u>blue</u>. Write your answer in the box.

[ ]

3. How did the soldiers know where to find Jesus? Write your answer in the box.

[ ]

4. Reread paragraph 6. Jesus died on the cross so that we can go to heaven someday. Write the word **heaven** in the box below. Trace the vowels in yellow and the consonants in orange.

[ ]

# Day 5

1 Read the story as an *independent reader* to someone in your home. Ask someone for help if you get stuck on a word.

2 Respond to the reading through *writing*. Don't forget to use the correct punctuation in your sentences and try to add some detail words too. You're an awesome writer!

On the lines below, write about the following: What is the message or lesson of this story? How does it make you feel?

_____

_____

_____

_____

_____

_____

_____

Make it your goal to write at least three sentences. After you finish your sentences, read them aloud to someone in your home.

# Day 6

*Skills: Illustrations and Comprehension, Text Features*

Use your writing tools to *draw and color a picture*. The Bible tells us there were three crosses on a hill. Jesus' cross was in the middle. Draw a picture of three crosses on a hill. After drawing your picture, write a *caption* under your illustration that talks about Jesus' love for us.

Write your caption in the box below.

### Fluency Check

Set the timer for one minute, and see how many words in the passage you can read correctly. You are a Mighty Reader!

# Jesus and the Empty Tomb

## *Vocabulary*

The list of words below will be in the story. Take a few minutes to discuss the meanings of these words with your child before beginning to read. Ask your child to repeat them to you and use them in a sentence.

tomb: a place to bury a body

miracle: an amazing thing that cannot be explained

amazed: in wonder about something

risen: gotten up; come alive

appeared: came into sight

Biblical terms: Jesus, Peter

## *Skills*

Refer to the Reading Skills Guide on page 7 for a detailed explanation about many of these skills.

Key Details

Context Clues

Punctuation

Phonics

Connecting Writing with Reading

Text Features—Captions

Vocabulary

# Jesus and the Empty Tomb

*from Matthew 28:1–8; Luke 24:1-49*

1. After **Jesus** died, He was put in a **tomb**. A big stone was rolled in front of the doorway. Many people were sad. But they were not sad for long. Three days later, there was a **miracle**!

2. That morning, some women went to the tomb. When they got there, they were **amazed**! The stone had been rolled away. The tomb was empty!

3. The women went inside the tomb. Where was Jesus? Then they saw two angels. They were scared. The angels told them not to be afraid.

4. The angels told the women that Jesus was not there. He had **risen**! He was alive! The women were so excited! They ran to tell Jesus' friends right away.

5. Jesus' friend **Peter** went to the tomb too. He wanted to see it for himself. When he went in, he saw that Jesus was gone. Jesus really was alive!

6. Later, Jesus **appeared** to His mother, Mary. He also appeared to His friends. They were filled with joy. This was a BIG miracle!

**Let's celebrate, Mighty Reader!**

# Day 1

*Skills: Key Details, Context Clues*

1   Read the story as an *echo read* with someone in your home.

2   Reread paragraph 1. Where was Jesus placed after He died? Underline evidence in <u>yellow</u> to show where you found your answer. Write your answer in the box.

3   Reread paragraph 2. What happened to the stone in front of the tomb? Underline evidence in <u>red</u>. Write your answer in the box.

4   Circle the word amazed in the text. What do you think the word amazed means? Write your answer in the box.

# Day 2

## Skills: Punctuation, Inferencing, Key Details

1 Read the story as a *choral read* with someone in your home.

2 Reread paragraph 3. Can you find the question? Write the question in the box. Be sure to add a question mark at the end.

3 After reading paragraph 3, why do you think the women were afraid? Write your answer in the box.

4 Reread paragraph 4. Why did the women run to tell their friends about Jesus? Underline evidence in yellow. Write your answer in the box.

# Day 3

*Skills: Key Details, Phonics, Context Clues*

**1** Read the story as a *cloze read* with someone in your home.

**2** The text says, "This was a BIG miracle!" Jesus had risen from the dead! Write the word **miracle** in the box. Trace the vowels in **orange** and the consonants in **blue**.

┌─────────────────────────────────────────────────────────┐
│                                                         │
│                                                         │
│                                                         │
│                                                         │
│                                                         │
└─────────────────────────────────────────────────────────┘

**3** What does the word **risen** mean?

O gone to sleep
O woken up, gotten up
O taking a nap

**4** Circle the word **appeared** in the text. This word means that something came into sight. Jesus appeared to several people. Write their names in the box.

┌─────────────────────────────────────────────────────────┐
│                                                         │
│                                                         │
│                                                         │
│                                                         │
│                                                         │
└─────────────────────────────────────────────────────────┘

# Day 4

*Skills: Key Details, Phonics, Inferencing*

**1** Read the story as a *partner read* with someone in your home.

**2** Reread paragraph 5. Why did Peter visit the tomb after he heard the news about Jesus? Write your answer in the box.

[ ]

**3** Reread paragraph 1. Circle the word **tomb** in (yellow). Jesus was placed in a tomb after He died. The word **tomb** is not spelled like it sounds. It has a silent **b** at the end. Practice writing the word **tomb** in the box. Trace the silent **b** in yellow.

[ ]

**4** Reread paragraph 6. Why do you think Jesus chose to appear in front of His mother and friends? Write your answer in the box.

[ ]

# Day 5

## *Skills: Connecting Writing with Reading*

**1** Read the story as an *independent reader* to someone in your home. Ask someone for help if you get stuck on a word.

**2** Respond to the reading through *writing*. Don't forget to use correct punctuation in your sentences and try to add some detail words too. Remember to focus and give it your best!

We can celebrate that Jesus is alive all year long. We often celebrate this special day at Easter. Answer these questions on the lines below: Why do we celebrate Easter? What do you love about Jesus?

_____

_____

_____

_____

_____

_____

_____

Make it your goal to write at least three sentences. After you finish your sentences, read them aloud to someone in your home.

# Day 6

Use your writing tools to *draw and color a picture* of the empty tomb. The tomb would have been like a stone cave. Don't forget the big stone outside of the tomb. After drawing your picture, write a *caption* under your illustration that relates to your drawing.

Write your caption in the box below.

### Fluency Check

Set the timer for one minute and see how many words in the passage you can read correctly. You are a Mighty Reader!

## Read:

But the fruit of the Spirit is love, joy, peace, patience, kindness, goodness, faithfulness, gentleness, and self-control.—Galatians 5:22–23

## Remember:

In Galatians 5:22–23, the Fruit of the Spirit compares our life to a tree that grows fruit. When a tree is healthy, it is full of fruit. Imagine your life as a fruit tree, except the fruit on your tree represents character traits such as love, patience, kindness, and gentleness. When you stay close to God through prayer and Bible study, people will see the fruit (these good character traits) in your life. Remember, Mighty Reader, spending time studying your Bible can help you grow into a stronger reader, but most importantly, it can help you grow closer to God!

## Think:

1. Which Bible story in this workbook was your favorite? Why? What can you learn from it?

2. Reread the fruits of the spirit in Galatians 5. Can you think of three Bible stories that give examples of them?

3. Which fruits of the spirit are easier for you to show? Which are harder?

4. Jesus wants us to show kindness to others. What is a way you can show kindness to a friend?

5. Self-control can be hard at times. How can you show self-control when you are at school?

6. When is the last time someone showed love to you? Have you shown love to that person too?

BE KIND TO OTHERS